About This Book

Title: *Hats*

Step: 1

Word Count: 75

Skills in Focus: All short vowels

Tricky Words: have, brims, fancy, straw, that, fur, flat, front

Ideas For Using This Book

Before Reading:
- **Comprehension:** Look at the title and cover image together. Ask readers what they know about hats around the world. What new things do they think they might learn in this book?
- **Accuracy:** Practice saying the tricky words listed on page 1.
- **Phonemic Awareness:** Have readers look at the word *hat*. Practice taking apart and putting together the sounds. Ask readers to tap a new finger to their thumb to count the sounds they hear. Ask: How many sounds are in the word *hat*? What is the first sound? Middle sound? Ending sound? Change the /h/ to /m/. What word is it? Repeat with the word *sat*. Change the /s/ to /b/. Ask students to name other *-at* words they know.
- **Vocabulary:** Briefly explain to readers that to *don* means to put something on, such as clothes or a hat.

During Reading:
- Have readers point under each word as they read it.
- **Decoding:** If readers are stuck on a word, help them say each sound and blend the sounds together smoothly. Be sure to point out any short vowel sounds.
- **Comprehension:** Invite students to talk about what new things they are learning about hats while reading. What are they learning that they didn't know before?

After Reading:
Discuss the book. Some ideas for questions:
- Do you own a hat? What kind of hat is it?
- What do you still wonder about hats around the world?

Hats

Text by Laura Stickney

Reading Consultant
Deborah MacPhee, PhD
Professor, School of Teaching and Learning
Illinois State University

PICTURE WINDOW BOOKS
a capstone imprint

Kids can put on lots of hats.

Kids can pop on caps.
Caps have bills in front.

Sun hats have big brims.

Put sun hats on.

Sit in the hot sun.

Don a red fez.
It is flat on top.

Put on fancy hats. Put pins, nets, or buds on hats.

Pop on top hats.

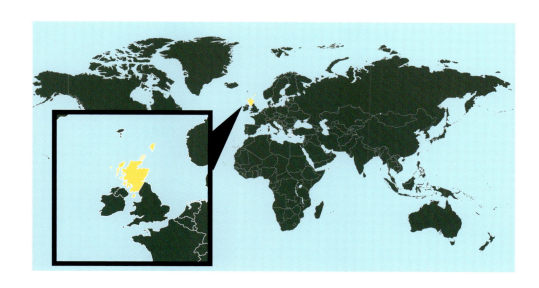

Put on tams.

Kids can put on straw hats.

Kids can don fur caps.

Pick hats that fit.
Hats rock!

More Ideas:

Phonemic Awareness Activity

Practicing Short Vowels:
Say a short vowel story word for readers to practice segmenting the sounds. Tell readers to hop in place as they break apart the word, with one hop for each sound they say. Begin with *hat*. They will hop once for /h/, again for /a/, and once more for /t/. Ask: What sound was first? What was the middle sound? Ending sound? Optional: Readers can clap or tap for each sound.

Suggested words:
- pick
- pop
- cap
- fit
- sun

Extended Learning Activity

Design a Hat:
Ask readers to design their own style of hat. Have them draw a picture of the hat on a piece of paper. Then ask readers to write a sentence about their hat. Have students use words with short vowel sounds in their sentence.

Published by Picture Window Books, an imprint of Capstone
1710 Roe Crest Drive, North Mankato, Minnesota 56003
capstonepub.com

Copyright © 2026 by Capstone.
All rights reserved. No part of this publication may be reproduced in whole or in part, or stored in a retrieval system, or transmitted in any form or by any means, electronic, mechanical, photocopying, recording, or otherwise, without written permission of the publisher.

Library of Congress Cataloging-in-Publication Data is available on the Library of Congress website.

ISBN: 9798875226953 (hardback)
ISBN: 9798875229206 (paperback)
ISBN: 9798875229183 (eBook PDF)

Image Credits: iStock: AbimelecOlan, 4–5, Erik Gonzalez Garcia, cover, FG Trade, 22–23, Frazao Studio Latino, 10, Gelpi, 16, hadynyah, 1, 18–19, MOcean100, 8–9, monkeybusinessimages, 6–7, 24, serge-75, 17, zoff-photo, 11; Red Line Editorial: 7, 13, 15, 17, 19; Shutterstock: Diane Bondareff, 14–15, Giulio_Fornasar, 20–21, Hatice Bakcepinar, 12–13, kornnphoto, 2–3

Printed and bound in Malaysia. 6274